D1710365

BIGGEST NAMES IN SPORTS

WITHDRAWN

JAMES HARDEN

BASKETBALL STAR

by Matt Scheff

FOCUS READERS

WWW.FOCUSREADERS.COM

Focus Readers is distributed by North Star Editions:
sales@northstareditions.com | 888-417-0195

Produced for Focus Readers by Red Line Editorial.

Photographs ©: LM Otero/AP Images, cover, 1; Bob Levey/AP Images, 4–5, 7; Max Becherer/AP Images, 9; Darryl Dennis/Icon Sportswire, 10–11; Marcio Jose Sanchez/AP Images, 13; Nati Harnik/AP Images, 15; Seth Wenig/AP Images, 16–17; Patrick Semansky/AP Images, 19; Mike Ehrmann/AP Images, 21; John Bazemore/AP Images, 22–23; Sue Ogrocki/AP Images, 24; Eric Christian Smith/AP Images, 27; Red Line Editorial, 29

ISBN
978-1-63517-487-8 (hardcover)
978-1-63517-559-2 (paperback)
978-1-63517-703-9 (ebook pdf)
978-1-63517-631-5 (hosted ebook)

Library of Congress Control Number: 2017948067

Printed in the United States of America
Mankato, MN
November, 2017

ABOUT THE AUTHOR

Matt Scheff is an artist and author living in Alaska. He enjoys mountain climbing, deep-sea fishing, and curling up with his two Siberian huskies to watch basketball.

TABLE OF CONTENTS

CHAPTER 1

NEW YEAR'S PARTY

It was New Year's Eve, and James Harden was having a party. The star guard was all over the court. His Houston Rockets were taking on the New York Knicks in a 2016 regular-season battle.

Harden took control of the game early. He made powerful drives to the basket. He hit finesse shots from long distance.

Harden launches a three-pointer over Knicks guard Derrick Rose.

And when he wasn't shooting, he was dishing out perfect passes to teammates. He crashed the boards to collect **rebounds**, too.

Harden piled up stats all night long. He completed a **triple-double** 10 minutes into the third quarter. And he just kept going.

THE BEARD

Harden is known as much for his facial hair as for his basketball talent. Harden's big, bushy beard has become his trademark feature. Harden says he stopped shaving in high school, and the beard has taken on a life of its own ever since. Fans love the beard. To honor Harden, they chant "Fear the beard!"

Harden (13) drives to the basket against the Knicks.

Despite Harden's amazing efforts, the game remained close. New York pulled to within three points in the fourth quarter. But Harden wasn't about to let his team lose. He drew a foul and drained his **free throws** on the next possession.

Then he zipped a pass to teammate Ryan Anderson for a three-point shot. That extended Houston's lead to eight points.

Harden didn't let up. With just over a minute to play, Harden set up behind the three-point line. Anderson passed him the ball. Harden launched a shot from deep. The crowd roared as the ball swished through the net.

Harden had 53 points for the night. It was the highest total of his career. It also tied the all-time record for most points scored in a triple-double.

The final seconds ticked away on the Rockets' 129–122 victory. By then, Harden had notched a career-high

Harden's amazing stats earned him a trip to the 2017 NBA All-Star Game.

17 **assists** and season-high 16 rebounds. He was the first player in the history of the National Basketball Association (NBA) to have at least 50 points, 15 assists, and 15 rebounds in one game. Harden's incredible performance left fans, coaches, and fellow players in awe.

CHAPTER 2

EARLY LIFE

James Edward Harden Jr. was born on August 26, 1989, in Los Angeles, California. His father, James Sr., was in the US Navy. But he was not a part of young James's life. He had problems with drugs and spent time in prison. James lived with his mother, Monja Willis, in the city of Compton, California.

A young James Harden participates in a basketball camp in 2006.

James's mother was not strict. She let James make his own mistakes. But she was there for him when he needed help. If she thought her son was on the wrong path, she gave him advice.

Compton was known for having a lot of crime and gang activity. Monja did not want him getting caught up in any of those things. So, she sent him to Artesia High School in nearby Lakewood, California. She didn't realize it at the time, but she was sending her son to a school that was a basketball powerhouse.

James was a gifted athlete. He loved playing basketball. But there was little reason to think he would become great.

Harden leaps over defenders in a 2008 game against Stanford.

As a freshman in high school, he stood 6 feet 1 inch (185 cm) tall. That wasn't small, but it wasn't big for a top-level basketball player. James also suffered from **asthma**. He needed frequent rests just to catch his breath. He always carried an **inhaler** with him in case of an asthma attack.

James continued to work hard. And he continued to grow. His asthma became less severe. By the time he was a junior in high school, he was the star of the team. He led Artesia to state championships in 2006 and 2007.

James was gaining national attention. Colleges around the country wanted him

Harden scored 1,309 points in his two seasons with Arizona State.

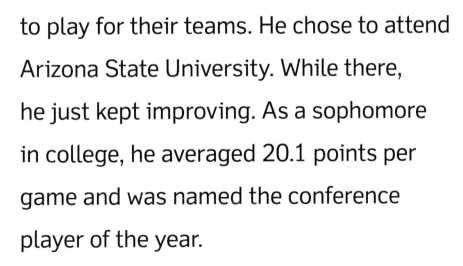

to play for their teams. He chose to attend Arizona State University. While there, he just kept improving. As a sophomore in college, he averaged 20.1 points per game and was named the conference player of the year.

CHAPTER 3

SIXTH MAN

After two years of college, Harden believed he was ready for the NBA. He decided to enter the 2009 NBA **Draft**. Harden was not the tallest player, and he was not the most athletic. But he was smart and hard working. Many experts ranked him as one of the top players available in the draft.

Harden shakes hands with the NBA commissioner after being drafted by the Oklahoma City Thunder.

The Oklahoma City Thunder liked what they saw. They selected Harden with the third overall pick in the draft. Harden would be joining an up-and-coming team led by two young stars, Russell Westbrook and Kevin Durant.

GOING FOR GOLD

Harden was a member of the 2012 US men's Olympic basketball team. He played alongside teammates Durant and Westbrook. Harden traveled to London, England, with the team. He served as a reserve, averaging 5.5 points per game. With Harden's help, Team USA won all of its games and earned the gold medal. Harden won gold again for Team USA at the 2014 Basketball World Cup.

Harden battles for possession during a game in his rookie season.

Harden started out as a reserve. He was the Thunder's "sixth man," which means the first player to come off the bench. Harden averaged 9.9 points per game in his rookie season. He helped the Thunder reach the 2010 **playoffs**. The team returned to the playoffs in 2011.

They even advanced to the Western Conference Finals.

The Thunder kept getting better, and so did Harden. In 2011–12, Harden averaged 16.8 points per game. He was also named the NBA's Sixth Man of the Year. Even better, the Thunder advanced all the way to the NBA Finals to face the Miami Heat.

Harden struggled in the Finals, however. The Heat shut down his outside shot. With Harden struggling, the Thunder didn't stand a chance. Harden could only watch as Miami celebrated a 4–1 series victory.

The Thunder had lost the series, but their future seemed bright. Westbrook

Miami Heat guard Dwyane Wade dunks over Harden in Game 3 of the 2012 NBA Finals.

and Durant had already become superstars. Harden seemed only a step away from joining them. Few fans would have guessed that Harden would never wear a Thunder uniform again. Change was coming.

CHAPTER 4

ROCKET MAN

After the 2011–12 season, Oklahoma City offered Harden a contract extension worth more than $13 million per year. It was a lot of money, but it was less than the NBA's top stars earn. Harden turned down the offer. He believed he was worth more.

Harden had a fantastic season in his first year with the Rockets.

Harden chats with his former Thunder teammate Russell Westbrook after a 2012 game.

The Thunder then made a move that shocked many NBA fans. The team traded Harden to the Houston Rockets. Soon after, the Rockets gave Harden a five-year, $80 million contract.

Harden immediately became the star of the Rockets. In his first game with his new team, he scored 37 points and had 12 assists. It was just the beginning. Harden averaged 25.9 points per game for the season. He led Houston to the playoffs. But the Rockets were eliminated by Harden's old team, the Thunder.

Harden continued to grow into one of the NBA's best scorers. In 2013–14, he was named to the All-NBA First Team. Then in 2015, he led the Rockets to the Western Conference Finals. In one playoff game, Houston was clinging to a one-point lead. Harden had the ball with only 12 seconds left. In a flash, he launched a shot. The ball rattled around the rim and bounced off the backboard.

Then it fell through the net. Harden's shot secured the Rockets' victory.

The 2016–17 season was Harden's best yet. Harden seemed unstoppable at times. But the playoffs were a different story. Harden couldn't find his regular-season magic. The Rockets were eliminated in the second round.

POINT MAN

For most of his career, Harden played shooting guard. But in 2016–17, Rockets coach Mike D'Antoni had a different plan. D'Antoni played Harden as the team's point guard. The point guard is traditionally a smaller player whose focus is on ball-handling and passing. Harden thrived in the role.

Harden's skills should keep the Rockets in the playoffs for many years to come.

The season was over, but Rockets fans had reason to be optimistic. In the offseason, Harden signed the biggest contract in NBA history. Harden would be wearing a Rockets jersey for the next six years.

JAMES HARDEN

- Height: 6 feet 5 inches (196 cm)
- Weight: 220 pounds (100 kg)
- Birth date: August 26, 1989
- Birthplace: Los Angeles, California
- High school: Artesia High School
- College: Arizona State University, Tempe, Arizona (2007–2009)
- NBA teams: Oklahoma City Thunder (2009–2012), Houston Rockets (2012–)
- Major awards: 2009 Pac-10 Conference Player of the Year; 2012 NBA Sixth Man of the Year

Los Angeles

Oklahoma City

Tempe

Houston

FOCUS ON
JAMES HARDEN

Write your answers on a separate piece of paper.

1. Write a paragraph that explains the main ideas of Chapter 3.

2. Do you think the Thunder should have traded Harden to the Rockets? Why or why not?

3. In which state did Harden grow up?

    A. Arizona
    B. Oklahoma
    C. California

4. Why did the Thunder trade Harden to the Rockets?

    A. The Thunder didn't think Harden enjoyed living in Oklahoma City.
    B. The Thunder didn't think they would be able to afford Harden's next contract.
    C. The Thunder didn't think Harden was a good player anymore.

Answer key on page 32.

GLOSSARY

assists
Passes that lead directly to a teammate scoring a basket.

asthma
A medical condition that can make breathing difficult.

draft
A system that allows teams to acquire new players coming into a league.

free throws
Shots from the foul line worth one point each, given to a team after one of its players has been fouled.

inhaler
A device that delivers medicine to the lungs.

playoffs
A set of games played after the regular season to decide which team will be the champion.

rebounds
Plays in which a player controls the ball after a missed shot.

triple-double
A game in which a player has double-digit numbers in three categories. The categories are often points, assists, and rebounds.

TO LEARN MORE

BOOKS

Fishman, Jon M. *James Harden*. Minneapolis: Lerner Publications, 2016.

Trusdell, Brian. *James Harden*. Minneapolis: Abdo Publishing, 2017.

Whiting, Jim. *Houston Rockets*. Mankato, MN: Creative Education, 2017.

NOTE TO EDUCATORS

Visit **www.focusreaders.com** to find lesson plans, activities, links, and other resources related to this title.

INDEX

Answer Key: **1.** Answers will vary; **2.** Answers will vary; **3.** C; **4.** B